AF326707

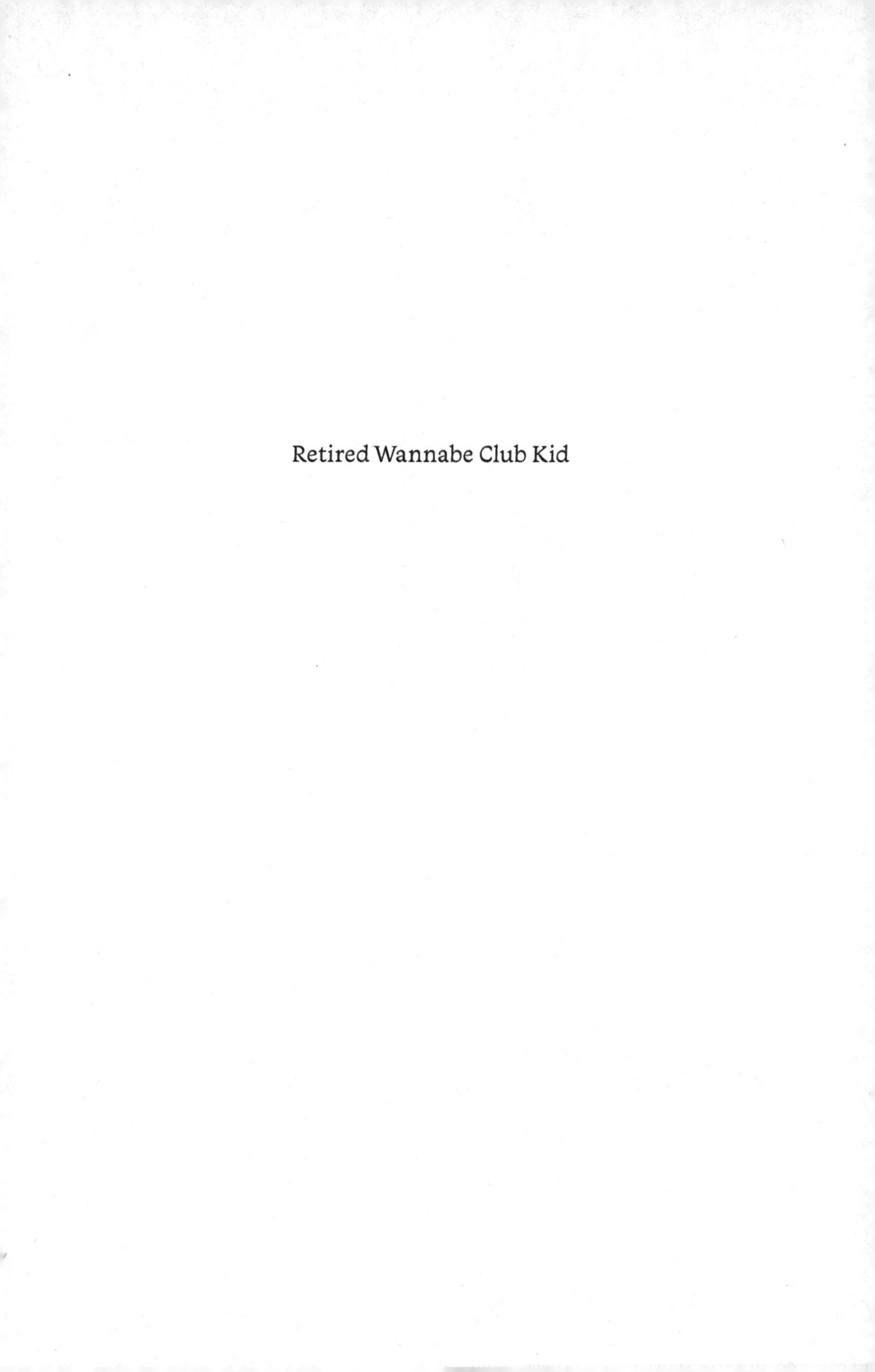

Retired Wannabe Club Kid

Retired Wannabe Club Kid

Rachel Turney

Content warning:
This collection references drug and alcohol use
and talks about some dubious situations.

Parlyaree Press
Atlanta, Georgia
www.parlyaree.com

Library of Congress Cataloging-in-Publication Data
Names: Turney, Rachel, author.
Title: RETIRED WANNABE CLUB KID / Rachel Turney
Description: First Edition | Atlanta : Parlyaree Press, 2026
Identifiers: LCCN: applied for | ISBN 978-1-961206-31-1 (hardback)
Subjects: LCGFT: Poetry
LC record available at https://lccn.loc.gov/

Design by Parlyaree Press
Cover Photo by Rachel Turney

Front Cover/Title Typeface is Banana & Aviano Flare.
Interior Title Typeface is Park Lane. Text Typeface is Monarcha.

Hard Cover ISBN: 978-1-961206-31-1

Ebook ISBN: 978-1-961206-32-8

To: My Caribbean Dream.

Foreword from the Poet:

When I was 14, I found the beat and never lost it. I was what some call a "wild child", which is a lame thing to label a kid. After very much enjoying my 13th and 14th year, I was cruelly imprisoned in a tower of servitude with the Duggar family. (You can read about The Institute of Basic Life Principles, a sinister cult, online to learn more.) In 2001, I managed a great escape and went with my family (strangers by then) to Europe. I found myself again, in Eastern Europe in the freedom of border movement, nights, and anonymity. I went on to spend time studying in Poland and teaching in China. I also traveled extensively while working in education and hospitality. In 2013, I turned my focus primarily to my career; and in 2021, I met my sputnik while minding my own business in the Caribbean. Now, I am Jane Jetson living in the suburbs, but I have a killer sound system. This collection is about my journey as a party girl and wannabe Club Kid. The true Club Kids were partying in New York City and globally about a decade or two before I came on the scene, my greatest lament. This is an homage to them, to nightlife, and to the freedom I hope we all find. To every young woman, young man, and all the other kids who put on their eyeliner a little crooked and felt terribly misunderstood - this is for you.

P.S. What I really want is for someone to make this into an EDM/house/techno album. If you are interested in a collaboration, please contact me.

RETIRED *wannabe* CLUB KID

STORIES FROM THE INTERNATIONAL CLUB SCENE,
ODES TO THE BEST PARTY CITIES IN THE WORLD,
AND LOVE POEMS TO THE NIGHT

Rachel Turney

Contents

2013-2020 - Semi-Retired

1999
The New Millennium

The Fall of 1999

Back before it all began,
I wish I knew me then.
The same sky,
the same night.
I would have looked into my own eyes
and asked about the stars.

I was half horse and half human,
half girl and half moon.
I was an owl at night.
I was a raven at sunrise,
shapeshifter.
I was the freedom
and the coop.
I was the tanked fish.
I was the caged bird.

Set me free.
Set me free.
I want to fly.
What's out there?
I just want to know.

Pour me into the river.
I'll swim down the Mississippi.
Open my wire door
so that I can soar.
Do not sedate me.
Do not imprison me.
I am not a human,
don't treat me like one.

I am magic.
I am passion.
I am the night Goddess.
I am the future.
I am the expanse.
I am the space between the stars.
I am the midnight dancer.
I am a Club Kid,
let me shine.

The Dawn

We danced at night in parks,
never the same one. Always
moving, roaming Cervidae.

I saw myself in the cosmos;
I was invincible. I grew
wings and flew. It all was
possible then.

The little birds would sing.
The sun would come up.
Dew covered my body. I was
part of the

                                                  ritual of dawn.

Purity

I'm in love with the forest: filled with my friends,
and all the freedoms of the night.

I am guarded by the tree growth: I am tucked away,
confined to these few miles I can roam.

They mute me with pills and vials. They feed me
poisoned apples and tell me they are

for my own good.

I wake from my stupor, choking on the red rind.
I regurgitate it all: every pill, every prayer, every bite
I was ever fed.

But do not worry: your punishment will be dance,
forever in bright red shoes.

Perhaps it will all be

for your own good.

Be My Carbonation

I want a life with carbonation!
I want to feel the

    fizzle

            pop!

Dissolve me

               pressurized

bursting

          explode!

Compositional Layer

No sleep.
We don't need it.

Touch my body.
I am   electricity.

Drink me in,   liquid adrenalin.
The sound will take us   underground.
We can be free there.
The ceiling is   1,000 feet tall.

We are in the   inner core.
We will never   touch the blue.
Sailing on clouds   forever.
If we grew wings   tonight...

We are in a new dimension.

Redefining Night

We have redefined night.
      It used to mean dinner.
But now it's eggs and bacon.
      It used to mean darkness.
But I leave all the lights on.
      Sleep used to be night.
But now it is eyes wide open, tarsier.

We are the linguists of the shadows.
      We define the night.

A Waste of the Sun

I'm a sky full of light
and you are nocturnal.
Swim with me,
          in your eyes,
                    in your skin.
You leave me at dawn,
empty bed.
I am drowning.

How can you not see it?
It's the worst sunrise ever.
Noon is sorrow.
When will it be night again?

You let me go.
You let me down.
I could hardly float.

How could you not see it?
I loved you.
It's deprivation that your
skin isn't here.

Was it all a complete waste,
a waste of the sun,
to have loved you?

Incinerate

I don't need you.
I don't need any of this.
I'm fine without you,
because I'm the firestarter.
I'm the main attraction,
the architect of the night,
the producer of the sequence.

Watch me burn.
I'm the books you threw
on the flame.

I Know Why the Caged Bird Sings

I'm what you fear.
I'm bad, horrid.
I'm also very good,
making music everywhere I go.
I am a walking installation.
Don't stand too near.
I'm 3,000 centigrade,
the Egyptian sun.

Nocturnal Animal

I am the

nighttime,
nocturnal
echolocation,
I sing
to you.

bounce
parliament of owls

The night sets them free.

colony of bats
flying

I am onyx,
with shining emerald eyes.
I am stalking in the jungle.

patagium

Into the air I sail.
The reverberation of your
words haunts me.

I am laughing at the moon
with my head thrown back.
I am bioluminescent.

luciferin
a solar flare burning green
I am screaming at the darkness.

howling
nuclear fusion

      I light the night.

The New Millennium

There will be
hordes of eagles
soaring upward.

      The end of the
      world will come.

Chariots pulled by
horses made of fire.

      The wrath of god.
      The righteous
      will ascend.
      They shall be
      raptured.

            Not me, please!
            Leave me here!
            I want to stay
            right here,
            dancing.

Emergence

Don't turn on
the lights,
I pray to the sun.
Let it never end,
this dark.

The sand is cold.
I am spinning wildly,
silk round and round,
creating my cocoon.

How will I transcend
if the sun comes up?
How will I grow
wings, translucence?
How will I complete
my metamorphosis
if the night ends?

Tomorrow, I won't
be a caterpillar.
I won't be a butterfly,
I will be a girl again.

2000-2001

There was no music. There was no dancing.

2000-2001

There was
no music.
There was no
dancing.

2002-2003 Europe

Radio 88

bowl of cereal
walk a mile
cold classroom

        play guitar in a small room for three hours
        eight p.m. — two beers at the bar
        club opens at ten
        third story
        dance until the sunrise

alone at eight a.m.
bowl of cereal
listen to old techno
on Radio 88
start the day
just like all the others

Let Me In

Open up the door, let me in.
Invite me. Show me your home.

I'm in the garden waiting, a part
of me will always be waiting.
"You're welcome to come in."
But how long can I stay?

Will I be welcome back tomorrow?
Open up the door, you can be sure
I recognize you.

I only need a moment to breathe
the same air as you, to feel your
form near mine.

Lasa-ma sa intru.
Let me in.

Time Table to Outer Space

9 p.m.

Troposphere

3 a.m.

Mesosphere

11 p.m.

Stratosphere

6 a.m.

Thermosphere

Dopamine

Do you like what you are looking at?
Come and get some liquid dopamine.

What's this song?
Could you play techno?

I want to dance again.
Drop the beat.

I want to be barefoot in a field,
in the grass in the rain,
while I am standing here,
at the club with all my friends.

Can you make it more techno?
I'll tell you my name if you impress me,
or you can call me Valerie.
I am ecstasy.

I am D-1 and D-2.
I'll make you feel.
We can be locomotion.

Music Mosaic

All around me is music.

The notes all have colors.

a strobe light
a kaleidoscope

I am standing in the middle,
silhouette.

Every movement disturbs the glass,
shines off the mirrors.

I am a mosaic made up of pieces of the night
placed together and swimming in acrylic.

Add glitter and I shine forever,
a mosaic sculpture.

The Best Club in the World

In my dream last night, I was in that five-story club. The one in Budapest. You know it, I'm sure.

There is no melody in this club. Just rhythm. Each floor, its own beat. The first and second floor are for every party kid.

You can get a tattoo by a guy in a cage on the third floor if you know which door to go through. If you're into that kind of thing. I don't think tattoos should be done in barely lit places, but that's up to you.

The fourth floor is filled with clocks. They all read three. None of them tick.

This club has no name, but most people refer to it as Stories. You can call there to see if they are open. If your call goes to voicemail they are closed. If it rings and rings, they are open. They might be open at five in the afternoon, they might be closed at midnight.

An elevator goes to the fifth floor, opening to a door that requires a key. I've been there only once. It was by far the best place I have ever partied. You can keep Rio, you can keep Beijing, you can keep Los Angeles. The fifth floor of the club with no name in Budapest is the place to find the beat, find the rhythm.

When I Met Eve

Can't forget you standing there.

Dark eyes, long hair. Simple black skirt and white t-shirt. Did you invent how to wear clothes? Are you the first human to ever walk the Earth? Did you run naked in a garden, bite an apple?

Come back, I have more questions. Please don't go away into the night. You're a ship and I am swimming wildly. You are water when I am so thirsty.

I would give anything to touch you. The feeling of paradise. Let me caress your hair, your face. You are the stars, something I cannot hold. You are time. I could be your snake. Let me whisper what to do.

Board this spaceship with me so that we can be eternal. Let's go wherever it takes us, an adventure. You make me alive. You make me shiver. I feel everything now that I see you.

Can you feel what I feel? You are life, the living one. I am a sheep. I will follow you. You are the first and the last.

Every color we see in the night is so much different than what we see in the day.

The Other Side

The other side is filled with dancing, just like here, but

<pre>
   w   t   o   r   i   y.
        h   u   g   v
   i   t   a   t
</pre>

Run into my arms and feel my love. Close your eyes, listen to my voice, the beating of my heart.

Come with me to the other side. I don't want to spend one more moment, not a second, without you.

I'll make you feel the blood through my veins. Can you touch it? It beats to music. Would you want to be one with me?

I'll tell you all the secrets if you come to the other side. Don't stay where you are safe and sound. Listen to the music and fly away with me.

Be My Star

All I know is I can't leave here without you tonight. If you were an island, I would swim to you.

Don't leave me alone in the galaxy.

The sound of that one song floods me with memories. I feel like I am standing in a waterfall. Swimming in glacial waters. I am frozen in time, a time when I knew you.

I want to go back to when I knew you. When you were mine. Seeing you is torture. Am I wrong?

Tonight we can change it, make it right. We can get in a time machine and be in 2003 when every night was just you and me.

1/4

I like you:
your touch,
the way you move,
the way you dance,
how you are man
and you are woman,
how you are the phantom
and you are the angel of the music.

three hundred and sixty-five

You are:
the sticky dance floor,
the crystal chandelier.

I like you from eleven until five a.m.
After that I turn into a bird and fly away,
a small one that can slip through cage bars.

But until the morning, I like *you* for six
hours, the perfect balance and harmony.
You can have one fourth of me.

Bullet Beats

the music is a bullet
      ricochet
the music is a heartbeat
      cardiac arrest
words are chandeliers
      crashing to the ground
back beats are entrance lines
      pounding on the pavement
moving through time
      supersonic speed
deep patterns
      snowflakes, honeycombs, anemone
singing bowls and a stick hitting a plastic bucket
      tap shoes on a sprung floor of maple
waves against rocks and the tinkling of shells on sand
      percolation, a katajjaq duet

Europe

What's the best place to party?

Berlin.

Well, let me think about it.

Barcelona?

London.

Reykjavik.

Budapest. It has to be Budapest.

Warsaw.

Milan.

Riga, unexpectedly.

Helsinki.

Zagreb.

No, my answer is Berlin.
Definitely Berlin.

Green Pastures

Let me take you
somewhere you haven't ever been.
You won't remember it
but for tonight, it will be everything.

       bucolic pasture
       rave
       everybody
       round

Sand to glass and back to sand.
You'll feel alone again
but you have to let go.

In a world where you are free,
you cannot sink into silence.
The music is pulsing.
You can feel it bouncing
blood in your veins.

We are heaven and starbursts.
The night is a playground
of our childhood fantasies.

Remember me.

Come with me while I do what I do,
so uniquely green.

10 Years

In this moment, I am freedom.
You are the clear blue sky.
Stitch in the sun. Hold all the
stars and moon at bay.

I will rotate with you, together
we spin, day and night. The
sunrise, the setting, it's all a
cycle, an eternal system.

365.2422 days

Come with me on my
geodyssey. We are in
outer space, our journey
home.

3652.422 days

Nostos
Escape *Calypso*.
Destroy the jealous *Antinous*.
Oikos
Eleutheria

2004-2012
Global

Bad

I wanted to be good
but I needed to live.
I wanted to stay in
but I love the beat
of the music.

I love the stars
in the sky, the
way it feels to
stay up to see
the sunrise. I
love the night
in Berlin, the
strange techno,
the sound of trains.
The lights in Shanghai.
The streets of New York City at 3 a.m.

I wanted to be good
but I had to live.
Cocaine in Hong Kong just
makes you feel at home.

Black dress and
torn tights.
Write your number in
lipstick on my thigh.
I'll never call you
because
I'm a bad girl.

You're like the one hundredth
person I have met tonight.

London in a telephone booth,
basement in Budapest,
red-eye to San Francisco across the Pacific.
A bad girl never sleeps,
wakes up in the ocean on a catamaran
somewhere in Belize.

Bought heels off another girl leaving the club,
danced in her shoes all night,
threw my flats in the quay
because
I'm a bad girl
in Singapore.

Electrify me.
Try to impress me.
Acrobats unfurling from the ceiling,
I've seen it in Moscow before.
You'll have to do better than that if you
want to impress me.

Corazón

Where are the roses?
Where is my heart?
I am lost in the music.

Is there something to feel?
Surely I would know it?

Dónde está mi corazón?

I don't want your kiss,
if it's the last one.
I want to feel the same
always, amplified.

Let's let nothing change.
Tears can't wash me away.

There is naught in the middle.
You've taken it all away.

Fading are all the memories.
Your laughter has left my ears.

When you think my name,
I feel it. I finally know the pain.

Bring me flowers.
Bring me my heart.
Turn back on the music.

RACHEL TURNEY

Always Check Under Red Solo Cups

In the morning, I find cocaine under a Solo Cup.
Why did someone leave this here?
Can I have it?

A Second Date?

God. She was making out with me in the corner
of a bar in St. Petersburg. She was wearing black
lipstick and glitter eyeliner. Blue eyeshadow.
I told her I was an American and she whispered
that she didn't care, it didn't bother her.

What did that mean?

She took me by foot to an alleyway nearby.
She knocked with two knuckles on a seemingly
random door. No marking. We entered a room lit
by dripping ivory candlesticks. She took my hand
and led me through a hallway, past thick curtains
into complete darkness. We dined there in the dark.
She used her hands to feed me something tart and
sweet at the same time. She leaned over and kissed
me in the dark.

God was effervescent, ethereal, amazing.

On the First Day
she made the darkness and the light.

On the Second Day
she would create the sky and the water.

I hoped I would be there for that.

Clouds

I'm in the clouds. I flew here on my
own wings that I grew. I have nowhere
to be but here in the clouds.

I don't want to be anywhere but here.
Will you stay with me, here in the clouds?
Up in the atmosphere, our breathing thin.
It's cold.

It feels right here, in the clouds. We can
stay awake forever dancing in the clouds.
We can make a tornado with our twirling.

I won't leave. Stay with me for just one
more night in the clouds. You can find me
here, just look up. I am always here,
floating in the clouds.

Destination Unknown

Somewhere - we won't have any troubles.
Somewhere - that's not our home.
Somewhere - near the warmth of the sun.
Somewhere - your name doesn't matter
because no one can hear when you introduce yourself.

Say - yes.
Say - let's go.
Say - it's all you want
to dance with me all night.

If you give your best, I'll give you mine.
We can impress each other as our iridescent selves
in the moon glow.

Say - I will lead the way.
Be with me in the night.
Say yes.

Come Closer

Can you feel me shake?
                    Pull me closer.
A deep breath, it's all okay.
                    Close your eyes.
Midnight is just the beginning of a new day
when we will be dancing, part of the history
of the night.
Don't deny my touch.
                    Electrified.

Beautiful

I must have told her
one thousand times
that she was beautiful.

Did she hear me?
I said it in Mandarin
just to be sure.

美丽的

She smiled but
did she understand?
She was glitter,
everything bright
and sparkling.

She was the way
your eyes open
after that first sip
of matcha latte.

She was the pull
of the night.
I was water
and she was
the moon.

Visitor

Friend or foe,
if only for a
night or so.

Connection with
guest,
newcomer,
migrant.

       like you
       like you

Acquaintance I call
friend,
lover,
fellow.

Visitor here,
if only for a
night or two.

An Angel in the Night

She's the one dressed all in white. Sweat is
dripping from her chin, or is it champagne?

She looks wild. Feral. She's been dancing
for hours. Frothing at the mouth.

Her fingernails are talons. Her incisors
are fangs. Her lips are always red.
She drank blood, ripped at flesh.

Her wings span almost six feet.
Huge and ivory. They are made
of feathers and keratin.
Halo around the sun.

What happens if you
make love
to an
angel?

flowers

what's that sound?
can you hear it?
it's a thumping.
where is the party?
where is the night chaos?

take me there,
nearer to the night.
i don't want to miss it.

comme les premières fleurs du printemps

Orca

I watch and wait, gliding through the water.
I turn one side and the other, smooth over
my skin. I dance to the beat. I drink flutes of
                    champagne.

Don't disturb the water. You can be a silent
                    killer.
Black and white, a dream come true.
Something from memory.

Dangerous, I know you. We are yin and yang,
                    destiny.
You are water,
        life.

The Desert

Cactus spine,
Mojave Desert,
the trees

      k   m
a   b
    i   o.

cholla
yucca

I am a scorpion.
Your breath will be shallow,
rapid eye movement,
sweat,
feel my sting.

None of my words are games.
My red dress is the fiery sunset.
I withhold the rain you need so desperately
and leave you naked.
It's about to get cold.
Enjoy the stars.

Club Girl Astrology

Aries - She organized the trip to the club. This was all her idea and she is ten minutes late.
silver sequin thigh-length dress with white leather ankle boots

Taurus - She insists on taking a cab to the club, even though it's only four blocks away.
black t-shirt dress with Louis Vuitton pumps

Leo and Aquarius - They enter the club first to take stock of the evening.
see through slip dress in lavender with black thong and no bra with cowboy boots in metallic silver
blue wrap dress with silver ballet heels

Gemini - She has made five friends in the first ten minutes and found out that the cocktail of the night is called The Starcatcher.
bright orange slip dress with blue heels

Virgo and Capricorn - They pay for drinks and make sure each of us has one before leading a toast to a fabulous evening.
black long sleeve form-fitting dress with green suede platforms
navy sleeveless mini-dress with white leather booties

Scorpio - She gets in a verbal exchange with some guy who is bothering Capricorn.
black ripped band t-shirt with hip hugger jeans and boots, studded belt

Libra and Pisces - They suggest we not argue and tell the guy to scram.
gray velour slip dress with neon pink slingbacks
silver crushed velvet mini-dress with black pumps

Cancer - She suggests it's time to go home as the sun comes up.
denim skirt with flats and a white tank top, Chanel shoulder bag

Sagittarius - I'm in the corner booking a flight to Milan because the DJ told me there is going to be a big party at Tunnel Club tomorrow.
black sleeveless dress with denim jacket and kitten heels

Her McQueen

I'm a proud peacock when I walk into the room.
I'm wearing Alexander McQueen paired with
Christian Louboutin. They aren't mine - none
of it is. They belong to a Russian model I met in
Kuala Lumpur. We are in Tokyo now at a bar in a
high-rise. A very small bar, in a very big high-rise.
The shoes are too tight, but the dress is perfect. I
walk slowly and hardly dance all night so I won't
ruin this girl's Alexander McQueen.

Later, I peel the dress off and lay it flat across a table.
I leave a note:

Thanks for the McQueen. Thanks for the red bottoms.
See you in Paris dear, this time next year.
Bring Dior lol (but seriously).
Ciao.

Fantasy

I'm the fantasy.
Are you jealous?
My life is a jet stream,
a four-digit code in London.
Thanks for the drink.

I'm the obsession.
The eyes you can't
get out of your head.
See me everywhere.
I don't wear lipstick.
Shake an espresso martini.

I'll be at the airport
drinking an eternal
glass of champagne.
My lips are parted,
ready for takeoff.

The streets are empty
because the party
is underground.
Step into my virtual reality.
If Soho isn't happening,
let's fly to Madrid.

My eyes are half open.
I am soaking up the sun,
in the South of France,
swimming in the Ligurian Sea.

All of this is what keeps me alive.
All of this is the fantasy.

Nyx

She's got stars
in her eyes.

A Nebula.

Nyx, giving birth to
all that shines in the night.

There is nothing.

I will be sound.

Selene

drives a chariot of horses across the sky.
Her long hair is the silver of the reflected twinkle.

Her smile stops the sun.

KitKat Berlin

Everything you said
on the dance floor,
did you love the words
you worked into meaning?

Were you drunk?
Were you high?

Do you remember what you whispered?
Do you remember how you touched my arm?
Do you remember how dark your eyes were?

The concrete under my feet.
The cold concrete on my back.

All the buildings here are made of concrete.
All the nights are filled with whispers.

Take Me Away

I surrender.
                    The
            music   can
    have   all   of   me.

Maybe
            it
                    could
last forever.

                                What if
            our feet
are exactly   where they are
                    supposed to be?

Remember me
                    just as I am
            tonight.

                            I don't believe
in regrets.
                    I never   have any.

How can
                            it be real
            if it never happened?

Don't open
                        your eyes.

Hi Ibiza

I have a vision of you.
You are the color orange.
The taste of fizzy soda
on my lips, mixed with
chocolate.

I won't forget.
vives en mi cabeza
no lo olvidaré
I see you in slow motion.

I try to recreate. When
I am here. It is like I
never left. Like it was
yesterday turned to
today instead of last
summer.

I won't forget.

Ibiza always lives in
my head.

Ibiza en mi cabeza
hazme un martini

Give me a shot of
Hierbas Ibicencas and
sangria that I will spill
on the ground as I
dance.

Se Déplacer

Every move you make is water splashing in a great big ocean. You are the divine sun. You are a magician circling the waves. The cosmos obey you. You are god, tremendous and eternal. Scale the mountains, you are the sky. The fog roll. When you move, the day can begin. You control time and space. You are electricity through wires, bringing us the music. Turn it up.

Saint-Tropez. Call me tomorrow, if you remember. Champagne should always be free, in a perfect world. Put me on hold; play music. The air can bring you to me. When the wind blows, you should be getting closer. Leave Paris and be here with me. Leave Montpellier, leave Lille. *J'ai besoin de toi immédiatement à Saint-Tropez.*

Move.

Global (in 7 Steps)

1. A cosmo at the Marquee.
2. Berghain in the darkness.
3. Rock music at CBGB in 2006.
4. Crobar and cocktails in 2007.
5. Take me back to the cold nights.
6. To the strobe light and the disco ball.
7. Meet me at the fair.

Quick Change Act

We got kicked out of the absolute
best club in Seoul.

I don't want to talk about it.

We had to go back of course. By ten a.m. we were in chairs
in Cheongdam-dong, getting our hair dyed and cut. We
started the day with elbow-length hair and ended it with
tidy bobs, tucked under, very 1920s. I cried about it, but
we decided it was worth it. Hers was dyed blonde and
mine jet black. The dye stained my ears a bit - little black
freckles of ink. We bought brightly colored dresses. This
would throw off anyone, as we always wore black. That
night we drank whiskey out of small plastic cups on the
train, on our way back to Itaewon-dong.

Leave Me Here

Let go of me. I feel at home again here.
I am whole again. I owe it to the night.
To my friends. I don't ever want to let
any of this go. I hold the music in my
heart. The rhythm is in my soul. I have
lost myself tonight and I want to stay
unfound. You can understand me in
language and through dance.

Let go of my hand. Take your palm
from my back. I want to be wildly
twirling in the moonlight. You don't
owe me anything. No skin on my skin.
I need to be free. Just leave me here
in the music.

I can't let go.

Iconic Night

The night is a string of pearls over a black dress.
The night is Audrey Hepburn.

The future of fashion, intergalactic queen,
Grace Jones.

Soufflé, beads, and feathers,
Cher in Bob Mackie.

The night is a yellow plaid three-piece skirt set.
The night is Alicia Silverstone.

A flowing green dress, like a jungle,
Jennifer Lopez in Versace.

A fiery red dress all tied up with a bow in Paris,
Princess Diana.

A swan draped over a body, distinctly
Björk.

Jeans and ripped tank,
Diana Ross dancing at Studio 54 in 1979.

White cone bra cups,
Madonna on her Blond Ambition Tour.

An inflated black patent leather suit,
Missy Elliot.

Soho (London)

The room is gorgeous.

> *Gold leaf filigree*
> *Soft velvet*
> *Reds greens navy*
> *Black textured wallpaper*
> *Crushed fabric swans*
> *Three DJs*
> *Pimm's Cup*
> *Champagne with strawberries*
> *Wee spoons of caviar*

The air is cashmere.
The music is silk.
You are sumptuous leather,
perfectly cut fabric of the night.

Kuala Lumpur

My grandma called and told me not to do drugs in Malaysia. *Grandma, I am offended by this! I don't do drugs of course.*

48 hours later I was smoking a joint and doing a little bump at a bar on Jalan Bukit Bintang with a British guy I met on Couchsurfing. His main selling points were that he had a pool and a lot of anonymous seeming friends. It was 100 degrees, so the pool was necessary and I wanted to be anonymous, too. I went by the name Natalie on that trip.

That May it would rain and before the drops could reach the ground they would evaporate back into the air. I swam laps in the pool with another Natalie the British dude knew. I surrounded myself with Natalies who didn't talk about their lives and spoke a lot of languages. When men approached them, they chose a language from their lexicon the intruder didn't know. Once they spoke French all night and I could hardly pick up a word.

We had drinks on a helicopter pad in the sky at sunset, the Petronas Towers in the distance. There is a members-only club in that building but you have to know about it and be on the list. Me and the other Natalies were not, despite us inquiring with British guy and his friends, who lied and claimed they didn't know of a club in the towers. Everyone knows (eye roll).

Me and the Natalies went to buy batik and had skirts made. Little bitty skirts which we paired with white tank tops and heels for the night. Batik beauties in blues, purples, and golds. I miss those hot summer evenings with the Natalies.

Fame

I am world renowned for:

> *the party*
> *the music*
> *the glitter*
> *the dresses*
> *the lights*

I am here for the
standing ovation,
the applause.

I'm the most
popular girl
in the world.

Everyone knows my name,
immortalized by my reputation.
Nods of acknowledgement,
whispers of reverence,
hums of praise.

The paper shows me
leaving a nightclub
in Shanghai at 3 a.m.,
my hand to the camera.

> *Could we get a little privacy, please?*

Heaven

Heaven is the space between two stars.
I have mine and you have yours.
There is a heaven for every soul.
As many spaces as between the stars.

                eternity
                immortal

There is no rest.
Heaven is filled with music.

techno
EDM
house

                music

You are the space between the   stars.
The space between your   thighs.
Welcome to the   afterworld.
Visit my   between.
Welcome to my   heaven.

Remember

I have seen you here before. It was this time last year. I thought I had lost you. The scooter ride through the strada. What happened to the distance? It has disappeared and I can see you clearly.

> It's not too late.
> It's not too late for this.
> It's not too late for us.
> We can be free in the night.
> Touch me and remember.

Phoenix Dance

a terrifying display of great beauty
she rattles like a *güiro*, like a *cabasa*
she shimmers
sparkling scarlet, vermilion
tangerine, honey, fire
she ignites the room with her
white, blue, orange, carmine flame
potassium chloride
she spins in the air
an earth sunset, the entire planet mars
a lychee fruit, a cranberry bog
a maple leaf pirouette
coral on the seafloor
screaming pandemonium of macaw
she leaps, *jeté*
grand pas de deux

To the Edge

My heart wanted something more.
Run to me. Cross the distance.

You bring me right over the edge.
I feel alive with you.

I feel like I am swimming in cold water.
The lake is deep and your eyes are dark.

The horses run past us, up the hill.
We are standing in their path, daydreaming.

The sun spins wildly, but we are holding still.
Facing each other in the morning fog.

Come with me. Let's get right to the edge.
Stand, look down the cliff. Kick little
rocks off into the moonlight.

What are the bounds? What are the limits
when it comes to you? Maybe there is no
rein or bourn. Let go.

Oh My God Stephan

> *Has anybody seen Stephan?*
The morning came and went.

> *Has anybody seen Stephan?*
Out to dinner, tiny shrimp and linguine.

> *Has anybody seen Stephan?*
The day becomes the night and we are at some bar, then we
are at a club we have never been to. No one sees Stephan.
The second night, we go out to Portinatx.

> *Has anybody seen Stephan?*
On the third night, we go back to our favorite spot.
On a couch in the back is Stephan, dressed in all black,
just like four nights ago.

*Oh My God Stephan, have you been at Ushuaïa this
entire time?*

New Year 2009

The worst part about high-rise life in China is the fireworks. On story twenty-five they burst right outside your window at all hours of the night and morning, ringing in the new year. Summoning in the Year of the Ox. The lion-dragon dances through the streets. On the 15th day, we light lanterns and watch them float upward. From my high-rise, I can see all the lamps below me, floating, aglow. All of the dreams and wishes ascending into the night.

Brunch at Shangri-La

I went to visit my friend Robert (who went by Uncle Bobby at the time) in Shanghai. When I arrived, I found he already had guests. They were in the bathtub drinking red wine, and I saw three male asses running down the hall leaving behind a trail of bubbles. At dinner, Uncle Bobby introduced his friends Sven and Steven from Qantas airlines. Later, a third man in a collared shirt with a kangaroo emblem joined us for drinks. It was clear that Bobby didn't know this one's name, though I suspected Sven and Steven were names of convenience rather than accuracy as well. Uncle Bobby was a very forgetful man.

On Thursday, we went to Hooters. They have Hooters in Shanghai, or at least they did. I have no idea why we went there. We drank beer and ate wings with Sven, Steven, and the other guy. At night, we went to the club. We all wore boas and sat at a table in the back with a group of journalists for what they'd described as the only indie magazine in China. We danced on the speakers and drank champagne. Real champagne, I was assured several times. We ate dumplings at 3 a.m. and then went to brunch at the Shangri-La later that morning. It was the most opulent and fabulous brunch in the world.

Uncle Bobby is an elected official and lives in the D.C. suburbs now with his wife and kids. I bet he thinks of that brunch too.

Face Control

Don't speak English.
Be as Russian as humanly possible.

I take my mission seriously.
Empty room for ten seconds,
I count them in my head.
odin dva tri

Black dress,
coat with a fur-lined hood.
Coach Soho in my hand.
Lipstick and mascara.
A cat eye.

I look the part.
And they let me in.

Hours

We will never ~~fade~~.
The song may ~~end~~
but we will dance
all night.

The passageway is
always turning left.
How can I follow
the road? Is there
a map? Do you have
a key?

Lost is a condition
of the night. Don't
haunt me. I can't let
the music ~~fade~~.

les heures passent

The Road to Oz

I am more alive
in this moment
than ever before.
frisson

The sound of
your voice
makes me shiver.
frisson

It is gasoline
on a fire
already burning.
frisson

It is runner's high
at four a.m.
on a parquet floor
in heels.
frisson

It is every
neon light and
bright red lip.
frisson

The rising sun
and a train in
Brooklyn.
frisson

Sitting by
the Seine
and smoking
a cigarette.
frisson

I want the smile
from the dancer
next to me,
connection.
frisson

I want love.
I want to sweat.
I want music.
frisson

Yellow brick
roads and
shiny red shoes.
frisson

I have emeralds
on my mind.
frisson

Boarding a plane
on cocaine and
sitting still
for ten hours.
frisson

Give me more.
frisson

I want some
more.
frisson

Looking for Alice

Chased a white rabbit
or was Alice chasing time...

We can't find Alice.
Take one to grow.

Who will defend the knave of hearts?
Stand next to me.

Will I ever see you again?
We are on the streets of a town that doesn't exist.

We fly over the mountains.
Our eyes are teeth to chew the landscape.

I can hear the ocean.
I followed her here.

Waves crashing.
I can hear her voice.

But that was a long time ago.
My heart surrendered.

Now I can't find Alice.
Not in the ocean, not in the sky.

I knew all of this would happen.
I predicted it from the start.

From the moment I met Alice.
I could see it in her eyes.

Now I can't find her anywhere.

Before Technology

We didn't swipe to find.
We went to the club and *danced*.

Nothing was delivered.
Dance was deliverance.

When the rain fell, we got wet.
When the beat dropped, we *danced*.

Everything was mystery.
Sin was a wink.

Primordial Goddess.
Even Zeus feared the night.

Heart

My heart, it wants something,
but I don't know what.
I'm at the edge of discovery,
of knowing why the sun shines.
Right on the edge.

Is it almost night?
I can see the pinks and reds,
tangerine is my dream.

We will be the land.
The water will try to hold us
but we are boats unmoored.

floating

I surrender to the waves,
to the movement of the sea.
It is a drum pounding.
It is my heart beating.

Jump over the edge and you will fly,
Icarus sun, full moon night.
It's not too late, we can ascend.

floating

Treasure

Everything shiny is mine.
I keep it in my treasure chest,
which I have with me now,
at all times.

If you come with me,
I will let you open it.
You can explore everything,
try on each ring.
Let me drape you in jewels
and caress this velvet lining.

The night sparkles and so
will you, if you come

with me.

Cartwheel

Driving over
one hundred
on the autobahn.

River flowing — quickly, slowly.

Gothic embrace,
hold me Dusseldorf,
while I reach for the
stars.

You

I like you,
you taste like night.
The salt I savor on the tip of my tongue,
the bitterness before I swallow.

I like you,
the smell of you.
Sweat mixed with black currant,
a field of flowers and a wood burning fire.

You,
the feel of you.
Hard muscle and soft skin
pressed against me,
the rhythm of your movements.

Your voice,
low and dark,
mysterious,
a sound I have heard before
but do not remember.

Satisfaction

It is a room full of people moving at the same time.
A perfect martini, held by the stem. An embroidered
cocktail napkin at a bar in Bangkok. Red carpet and VIP.

Champagne poured all the way to the rim. The beat
dropping at one a.m. A waterfall in the middle of the club.
Chandelier twinkling in the night. The acoustics of Fabric
in London, The Other Side in Amsterdam. I want to be
absolutely lifted.

I don't need sleep and that feels good. I am so free. Freedom
is satisfaction. The look of high heels without the pain.
A perfect spoon of caviar. A perfect spoon of cocaine.
I want every satisfaction.

Dreams

When you're dreaming,
you're dreaming of me.
What if you could feel that
without your eyes closed?
You could if you came with
me. I'm up here though,
you'll have to get higher.

I can be all you desire.
I can be your dream.

Until the Music Stops

We won't leave until
the speakers burn,
until my heart is slowed,
until the rhythm doesn't
move us anymore.

I'll fly up in the air,
carried by thermals.
We won't leave until
the night ends.

We are fire, take off
your mask. Nothing
can control us.

We are the queens
of the night, the bonds
of nature, our kinetic energy.

I don't ever want to stop.
I will spin forever,
pulsar in the night.

Give me a cadenza.
I want to be the star,
fermata in my movements.

Don't let the music fade,
like the smell of cut flowers,
art on a sun-soaked wall.

2013-2020
Semi-Retired

The Alchemist

The wind blows. The music plays.
There is always time for these things.
These things that are always.

A little fun is what you need. Are you
mine or not? I don't care about tomorrow.
I want to know about tonight, the next
						six hours.

I don't need a man. I have the whole of night.
Spin me around. Breathe in.

I feel so good. The perfect mix of everything.
So fucking good. I'm an alchemist.

It's like I made the playlist myself. Crafted
every cocktail exactly how I like it. Grew the
poppies with care. I'm a chemist.

A composer, I created the music. I run from
keyboard to drum. I take the mic.

You can listen to my music always, if you are
lucky. It might be always or it might be just
tonight. You will know by dawn.

Inside. I am alive. Remember my name.
						Always.

House Party

Are you in the car?
Darkness is my only flaw.
The rain, it is freezing.

Here I am, in only a tiny black dress,
standing under the streetlight,
in the greatest city known.

Pick me up on the corner of 10th and Bleeker.
Turn on the seat heaters.

Let's go to Astoria.
Let's go to Harlem.
I know a place in Dumbo.

I need a ride to a house party.
Where strangers are also my friends.
Where we all belong together in the night.

Fire Escape

My mother recently called and told me she wanted to make a graphic novel. In the comic, she is a superhero and drugs are the villain.

I pictured my own graphic novel in which she is the villain and a fire escape is the superhero. I would probably write it while doing drugs.

In the Rain

You are mine – made of stars.
I see the whole expanse of you.

My wrists flick in dance,
feet tap, slap on the ground.
My fingers are butterfly wings.
I am a lioness.

I don't have an umbrella.
I hold cardboard over my head.
I smoke 27 cigarettes under the awning
waiting with you for the rain to stop.

Make Me a Drink

I like my Manhattan perfect. Can you make that for me? I like my margarita with salt. My tequila sunrise with pomegranate juice, fresh squeezed. I want my martini dirty, three olives. A lime wheel. Candied ginger. I want my bourbon with two ice cubes. I need a Zombie. Remember those?

Hypovolemic Shock

Is this what you wanted? Is it everything you ever dreamed about? The sun will know all of your secrets. The moon sees you; you will never be alone.

Daylight can't change anything. It can't make you belong here. When you are from the night. You should stay there.

Vampiric. Do you have a soul? Are you the darkness? I watch blood drip from your fangs.

You compel me with your voice. I invite you in. Plasma and cells, nourishment to you. But I am thrown into shock.

Nebula II

Roll your eyes at what I said,
as if you know more than me,
as if you have ever been more
than I could be.

I ran five miles and you run none.
You tell me I am not as pretty as I
used to be. How would you know?
My nose is perfect, but you find a
flaw. You literally point out that
my nostrils are different shapes.

I climb a mountain and you claim
you could too. But you stay at sea
level for the rest of time. You say
that travel is a waste of money,
but I have some to spare.

You think you are very big and I
agree, you are the biggest void
that I have ever seen.

I escape you * *protostar* *
I gather *hydrogen* and *helium*.
I am *planetary nebula* and you,
you are a *black hole*.

Lights On

Turn on the lights.

What's your biggest
regret? Mine is the
sunrise. You are silent.
I am beating.

The opposite of large.
I am not here for you.
Never lose control. To
hold you up and hold
all of me in. I am not
your skin. Grow your
own organs. Epidermis.

In the silence you can
see me. Or will I slip
away, quietly. I want
to be free. Release me.

I hope you're happier
now. Truly.

The Story of My Making

I was born from a star,
that makes me a celestial.
How dare you look at me;
I am no human.
(I will burn your eyes.)

I speak every language fluently,
like the rest of the cosmos.
I am stitching the stars into the sky,
on the fourth day.

I am molding friends from clay.
I am ripping ribs out of the undeserving
to make something more beautiful.

Snow

I live within a snow globe. The glittering snow falls around me in a repeating pattern. I am shaken and positioned. I live in a little plastic cabin with fake smoke escaping from the chimney. I look up.

The snowflakes are dancing wildly around my head, like whirling dervishes. The snow covers my skin and quickly melts away. Crystals, liquid prisms.

I leave footprints which are erased, buried in the snow and then reset with each shake. Shake me back to life so that the glitter snow may fall on me all over again.

I Will Be Sand

I am furious,
a lioness.

You can't push me down,
I am absolutely glorious.

Like trying to stop the sunrise,
believe me, I have tried.

Open your mouth and
I will fill it with gold,
turn you to stone.

Look at me and my snakes,
we are sssssseething.

I will be the sand that you can
never get out of your hair. I will
be the headache you can't shake.

When they open your brain, they
will find me, grains of sand in
your fatty neurons.

Then you and your doctors will
finally know what went wrong
is that you crossed me.

Tulum

The thump of the drums,
on the beach in Tulum.
Sangria sunset and a fire
            burning.

It's quiet and melodic.
The music isn't loud.
The sound is absorbed
            by the sand.

The second story club
plays perfect jazz.
Crushed ice cocktails.
Mint swims in frosty
            rum.

A swing set lets your
feet dangle in the water.
Anything could swim
between here and
            Cozumel.

bailar bailar bailar

When the morning comes,
this will all be a memory.
The coffee and the tortillas
will eclipse this night under
the stars. Don't ever
            forget me.

no me olvides

The Time

Do you know the time?
Can I have a light?
Is that your last cigarette?
Can I have it... and a light?

Food for the soul,
that's what music is.
It's making love in the waves,
twirling feet dancing in the sand.

I won't forget about it,
this night, I mean.
A flashlight beam in the dark,
the path I follow.

I imagine myself as a little girl.
I am holding a rag doll.
She has braids, just like me,
equestrian chic.

One hundred goldfish in a tank.
How I wish to set them free.
I want them to feel what I feel,
the lack of glass rectangle prison.

What time is it?
Is it after midnight?
How much night is left?
I just want to smoke one last cigarette.

Voicemail

Twenty seconds is
not enough to say,
but I'll try anyway.

I'm sorry about last night.
I love you. Will we ever
dance again?
                              Goodbye.

2021-2025 Caribbean Dream

Veni ad Me

How far would you go?
From California to Mexico,
Tasmania to Sri Lanka?
All around the world
to find me, to hold me.

Your home is made of
aluminum alloys and
titanium. Seek me in
the sand. Find me on
the coast. I'm waiting
on an island.

Come to me.
Come to me.
Come to me.

pilote de mon coeur

Miracle Macaws

I found you,
>What a fucking miracle,
>by the water.

standing by the water.

You were the sun shining.
You were the colorful macaws.
You were the cool Caribbean
on my skin.

Sweat on my face.
Sand in my hair.

Something I didn't know I needed.
Something I didn't know I could
want so badly.

Dive Bar

unanswered questions
gum under the table
broken pool stick
no soap in the bathroom

San Francisco is the color red,
bright carmine in the fog with
an indigo sky background.
The night never ends and this
never happened.

Skin

I can tell you that I want you,
that I feel like I need you here
beside me, touching me, skin
on my skin.

Don't let go. Your skin needs
mine. I know you want it as
much as I do.

When the lights turn on it
better be you next to me.
I want to hear you whisper,
I am here and feel your skin
on my skin.

There is no end to our time,
we are eternal, diurnal and
nocturnal, we have overcome
sleep.

You're the one. Tell me every
single thing. The skin of your
shoulder, I have to touch you.
I have to undress you so that
I can feel more of you
on my skin.

Ultracentrifuge

You're my centrifuge.
Spin me and I separate.
You're the rotor.
Tonight we are turned to ultra speed.
         the planets and the galaxies
High speed, spinning wildly.
A tornado born from the music.
A Ferris wheel I want to ride all night.
An illusion, a zoetrope.
        electrons

        photons
I'm a record, baby.
I'm a snowflake falling to the ground.
Watch me pirouette as I cascade.
I am a w
    a
     t
      e
       r
        f
        a
         l
         l
           crashing on the rocks.
       keratinocytes

Draw me out, I am cotton.
Tell me the story.
Catch me, I am a salmon in your river.
I revolve around you.

Blood

My head is filled with all your words,
all the little whispers from your lips,
your voice in waves, carried to my brain.

But I don't only hear you with my mind.
I hear your voice with my heart,
transmitted directly through my blood.
Feed my organs with your words.

The word *love* is folate.
I want you is my B12.
Whisper all of your desires to me.
Tell me how I make you feel.
Want is hemoglobin.
You are oxygen.

Amsterdam

The city is red and black
                    with thick green glass.
I sleep with my head to the stars
                    and eat *appeltaart* with cream
                    for every meal.
The night is a playground,
                    loud thumping,
                    electronic pull,
like the circling canals.
                    The sun comes up,
                    the train station busy,
                    even at five in the morning.

There is everything you could ever want in this
cosmopolitan metropolis.

A little green fairy helps me find my way
from coffee shop to *woonboot*.

Give Me My Manhattan

Give me the city at 3 a.m.
The buzz of 5th
As if the very sidewalk has energy

Give me ramen and beer on Grace Street
Give me a steak at Peter Luger
Give me a cold walk on the Brooklyn Bridge

Give me spiraling stairs and
Impressionism, Abstract, Realism
A drink and marching Madeline

The skyline and the park
A fruit stand in Chinatown
Bottle of beer in a brown paper bag on the train

I want the lights and noise
I want the spills of theatre goers
The curtains in the doorways in winter

Give me a canopied rooftop
A basement concert
Drinks with glowing neon lights in the bottom

A smoke-filled room
A circus
Give me Yes

Bushwick in blues and greens
A DJ
A sunken dance floor

A line outside a white brick building
Give me a catacomb of techno
A monolith of music

Portal to another universe
But make sure you return me to
My Manhattan

Almost Midnight

I'm at the end of the road.
Keep walking,
I've been waiting here for you.
You can walk here.

If your mouth is closed
how will you eat?
If your eyes are closed
how will you know me?

Sizzling fat and hibiscus.
Is there time for us?
The heat from my hands.

Be delicious.
Eat your fill.
Take my hands in yours.
Scoop a spoonful of stars from the sky.
We will return them to the ocean.

I can see Saturn by the moon.
I taste salt on your lips.
Our feet are in the water.
It is almost midnight.

Life Is Simple

If you don't like it, change it.
Life is simple.
It's just night after night.
Your body moving in the moonlight.

Jump into my kaleidoscope.
We merge and refract.
Life is simple.
It's just movement, lights, and music.

Don't be sad.
Not a single tear.
What's actually worth it?
Life is simple.

When the sun touches your face, you are radiant.
You put one foot before the other, that's how it works.
Fry an egg, brew coffee — pour, stir, add cream.
Life is simple.

If you lose your breath, try harder.
Gasp for it; take it.
Never let it go.
Life is simple.

Put a brick on the pile.
You need mortar and a leveler.
See it's simple.
Life is simple.

Green Coupes

I like green cocktail glasses. They make me think of potions I made as a child. Little tonics in delicate bottles, labeled. Droppers used to add a bit of this and a bit of that. Today, I use a metal cup to measure gin and Lillet Blanc. I squeeze lemons and limes with a countertop whirring machine. I drop in a Luxardo cherry, a mini-luxury. I shake this all with ice-maker cubes and strain it over small green glasses. Twelve for 11.99 at the thrift store on 136th. Little green coupes filled with my concoctions. Only now, I share them with others instead of hoarding my potions in a little box and playing all alone.

Papyrus

Reach up. You are the light
in the sound. Touch me.

I am written on papyrus, a
whole history in hieroglyphics,
pictures and symbols
to say who I was.

A quill in ink upon my skin,
capturing a moment in history
that I can never escape.

You are near me, ecstasy, a
whole expanse in front of me,
next to me.

Touch my skin to read the story.
It is scratched there, in little lines
and figures. Read me row by row.

Drink Me

Drink me and I will make you grow.
I am an elixir. I am the fountain of
youth. I am water from Lake Mashu.

I am green tea, Hokkaido milk, and
coffee. A shot of wheatgrass. I am
The Reach on your lips. Don't waste
a single

       d
       r
       o
       p.

Drink me and I will strengthen your
roots. In your core you will know me.
Consume me. I am the radix.

Drink me and I will give you the
brightest flowers. You will be begonia,
peony, hibiscus, and hyacinth. Taste me.
I am a bite of katemfe fruit. The sweetest
thing you will ever know.

Polaris

You are my true north. I won't follow the magnets.
I forsake my compass. I don't need it. I'll find you,
Polaris.

In the shadows, that's how I will locate you. I can
feel you. You are constant. A globe point that never
changes.

You are the nail that holds it all in place. Without you
the world crumbles. Without you the needle moves and
the music stops. *Sois mon étoile du nord.* That's what I
will whisper when I find your ear.

Where Were You

When I was young, where were you?
Why are we meeting only now?
History is cruel.

Were you here in this ocean the whole time?
Could you not have grown legs and walked out?
I will stay with you now.
I will carve gills in my sides so that I can talk
to you under the water where you live.

Were you an octopus, with nine brains
and three hearts, changing color to camouflage
and intimidate? No wonder I couldn't find you.

Were you a twirling sea angel, your parapodia
useless on the sand? I wish I had known —
I also love to dance in the dark.

Where were you when I was a bird?
Why weren't you up in the sky with me?
Did someone cut your wings?

Alive, were you alive the whole time?
I don't know if I believe you.
Can you come back to me?
Crawl out of the sea, spread your arms,
jump and F L Y.

I wish the sun would set so that I could be
in the darkness, alone with you.
Just the two of us and the stars.
Where were you when I was an astronaut?
I couldn't find you in the whole galaxy.

Where were you when I was the sun?
I tried to spot you. Did you hide in shadows?
Were you lurking on the seafloor, my sea butterfly?

Where were you when I was the moon?
Were you afraid of the night?
A songbird, tiny in a nest waiting for me
to make way for the sun?
Let me make you free, little songbird, little songbird.

Be My Caribbean Dream

Desire, it might as well be a four-letter word.
Topaz against your skin.
You taught me how to swim again.

I could see color.
Had it all been black and white?
Your heart, I can hear it beating.
It is the most beautiful music.
The most amazing symphony in your chest.

Be my *American Boy.*
Climb into my head.
Swim there with the rainbow fishes.
Sweep away the sand.
There is no border in my mind.

Your eyes, the water.
Spin me in the warmth of evening.
Whisper that you are mine.
Be my Caribbean dream.

Big

I am the E X P A N S E.

I take up S P A C E.

I command L O O K at M E,

S E E M E.

Change

Break out of the cocoon and fly away. That's all I want to do. I want to make you proud with my radiant colors.

I am a vine and I want to grow grapes for you. Big, full purple grapes in the north of Italy. Crush me with your feet. Press me dry.

I am a rainbow that fades away in the sky. Will you remember that you saw me?

Blossom and bloom like a whole field of tulips. You could pick me and take me home with you. Place me in a bit of water, so that I could be near you — for the few days I lived.

I can't undo anything. There is nothing I can change. If I could, I would become a raincloud and wash away the past.

I wouldn't leave the room silent. I would flip the record for you, so that you are always in the music.

I won't leave again. I will be constant like mountains in the distance and the beat of your heart.

2026
Officially Retired

please moon, don't let the night end, i want to stay here forever.

Memories

Sometimes I look for clues of who I used to be in my Facebook memories.

Red Wine and Golf Balls

I have never drunk red wine out of the bottle while hitting golf balls, but it doesn't mean I don't think it would be nice. In fact, I would like to. I would like to hit golf balls at night in the dark with no care where they land while getting drunk on cabernet.
Somewhere in California.
Somewhere in Arizona.
Somewhere in Scotland.

Shape Shifter

Circle. Fully encompassed.

Rhombus. Tilted and confused.

Triangle. Pulled in three directions.

Hexagon. *It's sexy, fun.*

Square.

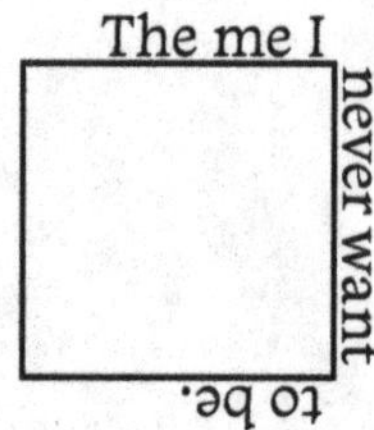

What's Left

What's left after the spotlight is shut off,
after the cheering stops,
after the music dissipates in the air?

What's left after the sweat has evaporated off the skin,
after the moon has floated away,
in the silence of the dawn?

What's left when I can't see the Hollywood sign anymore,
when the stars don't answer my whispering with their
twinkling?
What's left *after the glitter fades?*

Ivory Ice

Bite of red apple
Face of the moon
Whispers in the forest
Bird song and harmony
Hair that cascades like a waterfall
Like the stars that are agglutinated to the sky
Blood orange
Cherry juice on the lip
Poppies in the spring field
A rose plucked from a garden
Raw meat under the cleaver
Flecks of blood flying
Woodland creatures cannot save you
I open you like lychee fruit
Rosary beads
Say your last prayer
Your milky skin will be shattered
Porcelain vase
When you are poisoned and broken
I will be the *fairest of them all*

How to Live Like a Club Kid

1. Cast off your shackles.
2. Collect your name from the ground.
3. Reject servitude.
4. Embrace your ugliness.
5. Put on your eyeliner a little bit crooked.
6. Smudge your lipstick.
7. Cut open the wound and drain away the infection.
8. Count your white blood cells.
9. Tear your mirror off the wall.
10. Rip your jeans.
11. Write on your table with permanent marker.
12. Pull your shower curtain from the rings.
13. Leave a coffee stain on your white t-shirt.
14. Burn your bread.
15. Overwater your plants.
16. Talk to your neighbor a little too aggressively.
17. Live your life without exceptions.
18. Dance.
19. Dance.
20. Dance.
21. Never stop.

Notes:

Thank you to the following journals for previously publishing some poems from this collection:
"Give Me My Manhattan" - *Action Spectacle*
"Nyx" - *Suburban Witchcraft*
"KitKat Berlin" - *Azarão*
"Voicemail" - *Midnight Pantry*
"Take Me Away" - *Snoozine w/As Alive*
"Clouds" - *View from Atlantis*

The last six lines of "Nebula II" are almost the same as in my poem "Nebula," which appears in my collection *Record Player Life (the b-side).*

"What's Left": "After the glitter fades" is a direct quote from Stevie Nicks' song of the same name.

"Kuala Lumpur": Now I have three batiks hanging in my home in the suburbs. One pink one that I bought that same 100 degree day in Kuala Lumpur.

Acknowledgments

Thanks for the party. It was wild.

Thank you to Sean, Melissa, Lena, and Zach for the edits. Thank you to Parlyaree Press and Andrew for indulging me.

PSA:

Doing drugs from unknown providers in countries where use is illegal is irresponsible and poor global citizenship. Cocaine, cigarettes, and alcohol in excess are bad for you. Nods.

I'm gonna tell you the same thing I told my step-daughters. Drugs were different when I was a youth. They were "safer" in my opinion and we didn't have to fear fentanyl. It's really not worth it to do drugs these days. Sorry you missed the party. **Don't do drugs, kids. But do keep dancing.**

More From Rachel Turney

Record Player Life (the b-side) - The Poetry Lighthouse
To Be (a Woman) - redrosethorns
Women Making Soup Together - Vinegar Press

Founded in Atlanta, Georgia in 2023, PARLYAREE PRESS is dedicated to publishing writing that expands, reveals, and interrogates the mainstream. We seek out fiction, creative nonfiction, and poetry that exists in the liminal space between what was and what will be.

The cant of circus performers, freaks, queers, and thespians, Parlyaree is the invented language required to tell the stories of those othered, to keep their secrets, to keep them safe. It is a polyglot of experiences that may only be told in one's own voice. Parlyaree—as an invented language—borrows from what was to create something new.

That is what excites us at Parlyaree Press. Stories that transform; essays that reimagine; poetry that takes us behind the stanza to the core of our being and back again; language that plays as much as it conveys.

Writers: tell us your secrets.
Readers: reimagine your worlds.